THE KUWAITI OIL FIRES

SKIP PRESS

Artesian Press
P.O. Box 355 Buena Park, CA 90621

Take Ten Books
Disaster

Other Take Ten Themes:

Mystery
Sports
Adventure
Chillers
Thrillers
Romance
Horror
Fantasy

Project Editor: Dwayne Epstein
Assistant Editor: Molly Mraz
Graphic Design: Tony Amaro
Cover photo courtesy of Kuwait Oil Company
©2003 Artesian Press

All rights reserved. No part of this publication may be reproduced or transmitted in any form without permission in writing from the publisher. Reproduction of any part of this book, through photocopy, recording, or any electronic or mechanical retrieval system, without the written permission of the publisher is an infringement of copyright law.

www.artesianpress.com

Artesian Press   ISBN 1-58659-024-3

CONTENTS

Chapter 1

Red Adair had seen a lot of trouble in his life, and he had handled it all very well. He had been in the oil business for a long time, since the days when derricks—the tall stands holding up the oil pipe—had been made of wood. He came from Texas, where legend said that oil derricks were made of wood, but oil men were carved of steel. This could have easily been said of Red Adair, world-class oil field firefighter.

As he watched video shots taken over the oil fields of Kuwait, Red could see steel melt. It was a scene worse than anything he had ever seen. Six hundred oil wells were blazing in the deserts of Kuwait.

Setting the wells on fire was the last evil act of the Iraqi army led by Saddam Hussein. The thick clouds of black smoke that hissed and heaved from the flames threatened the survival of the entire Middle East environment, if not the world. Hussein's army had blown up 732 oil wells as they left Kuwait. Hussein said his army started the fires to hide from American fighter jets under the black smoke.

Luckily, all of the wells had not burst into flame, but most of them had. Now all that mattered was putting out those fires. Looking at all the wells burning was terrifying, a picture of hell itself. There were so many fires, it looked like a forest of steel trees, all burning. It looked like the devil's forest fire.

A problem this big needed the best minds in the oil fire business to solve it. A movie starring John Wayne had been made about Red Adair's life,

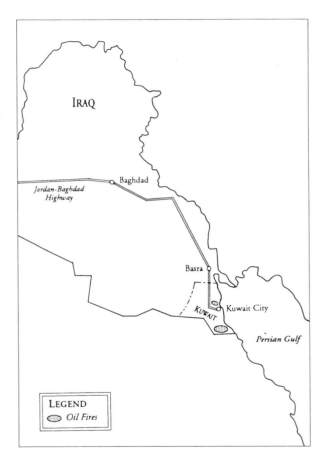

Saddam Hussein's army set fire to the oil wells in Kuwait, then retreated to Iraq through Basra.

called *The Hellfighters*. Now it was hellfighters to the rescue. Boots & Coots and Wild Well Control, both from Houston, Texas, joined Red Adair, Inc., while from Canada came the Safety Boss company.

Eventually, groups of experts from twenty-seven different countries combined their decades of experience and the latest in military know-how to put out the fires.

Normally, the only thing hellfighters had to worry about were the fires themselves. In this situation, the blazes were the results of a war, and many of the oil wells had highly explosive land mines around them. In addition, giant black lakes of oil had formed around some wells and on top of the mines.

As helicopters carrying the experts hovered over the awful scene, their thoughts were no doubt the same: this would be the most difficult job any of the hellfighters had ever faced.

Satellite images showed everyone the potential damage to the world's environment. The black clouds from the fires in Kuwait could easily be seen from outer space, and they were spreading daily. The oil fire experts, which included many top scientists and engineers, argued about how to handle the fires and remove the explosives around the wells. Getting everyone to agree on the proper approach was difficult.

News coverage of the war had been extensive. The United States Department of Energy did not want the same kind of reporting on the environmental impact of the fires, however. They took steps to see that news agencies did not make the problem seem worse than it really was.

To the hellfighters, politics did not matter. They didn't like continually informing reporters of their activities. The problem was very bad, and it needed their full attention.

The press continued to dream up stories. "Black Chernobyl," they called it, referring to the meltdown of the nuclear power plant in the former Soviet Union.

Saddam Hussein had called the Persian Gulf War the "Mother of all Wars." He was wrong, as his army lost very quickly. One report, realizing the task the hellfighters were up against, called the battle to extinguish the Kuwaiti fires the "Mother of all Smothers."

In the past, Red Adair and his men had usually done their jobs alone. This one, however, was far too big for just one company to handle alone. The country of Kuwait was very rich and could afford to hire as many people as necessary. But the Kuwaiti wealth came from the very wells that were damaged and burning. So the sooner the fires were put out and the wells were pumping again, the sooner the Kuwaitis could return to earning money.

The price of gasoline had gone up during the Persian Gulf War. That's because so much of the world's oil comes from that area known as the Middle East. Now that the war was over, prices were dropping. But as long as the wells were burning, Kuwait was out of the market altogether. Estimates were that six million barrels of oil—about a million tons in weight, worth ninety million dollars or so—were going up in smoke every day. In short, oil was being lost at the rate of one thousand dollars per second.

Even worse, if too much oil smoke clouded the skies of the Middle East, it could block out the sun so that crops might not grow. The climate itself might be threatened not only in the Middle East, but around the world.

All these facts added up to one thing:

the job had to be done very fast. The cost of doing it did not matter. Not doing it quickly and completely would mean a much higher price for everyone concerned.

Chapter 2

Although Paul "Red" Adair was not the first oil field firefighter, he was the most famous. He was the man who had developed most of the modern methods of fighting oil well fires. He got the nickname "Red" because of his dark red hair, and the name suited him perfectly. All of the cars and boats he owned were red, and he and his men wore red overalls.

In Red's many decades of fighting oil fires, he had been injured many times. The rims of his eyes were permanently red from exposure to poisonous gas. His skin had been burned too many times to count. Still, at the age of seventy-five, he was now helping fight the biggest oil field fire he had ever seen.

Red had come up with almost all of the methods used to put out oil field fires. By holding tin shields between himself and the fire, Red would get as close to each flame as possible to see what needed to be done to stop it.

The burning wells of the Kuwaiti fires sent flames and deadly gas four hundred feet into the air. The 4,000-degree temperatures produced by the fires made the sand around the wells so hot that it turned to liquid glass. To make matters worse, the temperature in Kuwait was 120 degrees during the day.

"The ground is so hot, if you kneel on it, you get blisters," said firefighter Mark Badick. Another crew chief said, "Your clothes heat up and your zipper burns."

Another danger was left by Saddam Hussein's army. Every well was surrounded by explosives and land mines.

American firefighters use sheets of metal as covers to approach the blaze of a burning oil well.

The smoke in the air was so thick and black that car headlights went on in Kuwait City every day by noon. One worker from the Safety Boss company said the sky was "darker than the inside of a cow." Another man said that breathing the air felt like someone was standing on your chest all the time. It was estimated that fifty thousand tons of sulfur dioxide—the main component of acid rain—was going into the air every day.

If ever there had been a place on Earth that was like the descriptions of hell in the Bible, this was it. One engineer said, "You half expect to see little guys with pitchforks and tails coming out of the ground." Another engineer said, "It's right out of *Dante's Inferno*" (the classic poem about an imaginary trip to hell).

Seen from the Landsat satellite, it looked like great black winds were painting ugly streaks across the entire

16

region. Plants were dying everywhere. The hospitals of Kuwait and nearby countries were filled with people having breathing problems. The pollution was compared to the worst ever recorded— in London, England, in 1952, when coal fumes combined with dense fog killed four thousand people in eleven days.

Richard D. Small, a fire researcher, said, "We have never seen a pollution event of this scale." Small said that the harm done to people, animals, and ecosystems in the region one thousand kilometers around Kuwait could be very bad. Smoke was reported as far north as Russia and as far east as Pakistan.

People around the world had been alarmed by the Persian Gulf War. Now, with the fires, the United States Department of Energy was worried about public upset over damage to the environment. They said that news reports were making the danger seem worse than it really was. Then they decided to stop sharing information, including satellite images, with reporters until the fires were out and the smoke was gone. Basically, U.S. scientists were under orders not to discuss the oil field fires with reporters at all.

The first great oil fire that grabbed the world's attention (and made Red Adair famous) was in Africa. The largest natural gas field in the world was in Hassi Messaoud, Algeria. Just south of that, in Gassi Touil, a gas well caught fire in 1961. It was burning 550 million cubic feet of gas a day when Red Adair was called in to put it out.

That burning well was nicknamed the "devil's cigarette lighter." The flame from it was so bright that John Glenn, the first American astronaut to orbit Earth, saw it burning from his space capsule. The vibrations from the burning well could be felt five miles away.

On that job with Red were his two top assistants, Asgar "Boots" Hansen and Edward "Coots" Matthews. Both men barely escaped that fire alive. If not for methods they had learned from Red Adair, they would have died.

While fighting that fire, Red and his men also had to deal with a war that was going on between French soldiers and Algerian guerrillas all around them. They also had to drill water wells five miles away from the fire to have enough water to fight the blaze.

Just setting up the operation had taken over a month. Pumps that had been specially designed by Red for the job had to be imported. By the time the job was over, there were three hundred men in the camp surrounding the fire. Red even missed the birth of his first grandson to fight the "devil's cigarette lighter."

Finally, just before noon on Saturday,

May 28, 1962, the "devil's cigarette lighter" was put out by tons of water sprayed over it. Then a fifty-gallon drum of nitroglycerin was suspended by a crane over the remaining flame and exploded, smothering the fire. This was another special method developed by Red Adair.

From then on, Red Adair was the most famous oil and gas field firefighter in the world. But the early fires were nothing compared to what the hellfighters faced in the oil fields of Kuwait. For everyone concerned, this would be the fight of their lives.

Chapter 3

Fighting the fires wasn't Red Adair's only job in the Middle East during war times. In 1973, his company put out blazes on an oil platform in the middle of the Gulf of Suez. These fires were started during a war between Egypt and Israel. During that fight, Red came up with the idea to use high-volume, low-pressure water pumps to put out the fire with only water, and it worked. It was the first time a water pump had put out an oil well fire.

Both the Egyptians and Israelis wanted the oil since they were at war. Part of putting out the fires had included getting them to call a truce and leave the oil alone while the firefighters worked.

With the oil boom in the Middle East came the danger of oil and gas well fires. Red Adair and other companies had been fighting oil fires there for decades.

Oil wells are drilled all over the world, in places of all sorts of geographical and political descriptions. So, the hellfighters who came to fight the Kuwaiti fires were used to just about anything. The Persian Gulf War was over, so there wouldn't be the danger of fighting troops nearby. But most of the hellfighters were used to fighting one, two, or even a few wells at a time. No one had ever seen anything like six hundred wells burning at once.

In the long run, the fact that so many hellfighter companies were called in to put out the fires would save the region. If two heads are better than one, in this case at least, many heads were best of all.

For once, Red Adair was not expected to solve the problem by himself. This was good. After all, he was in his seventies. He now managed his men from his office in Houston, Texas, rather than fighting the fires up close. He was a known leader with great wisdom, but because of the nature of the threat, a multi-nation solution was needed. In the same manner, armies from the free countries had united together to see that the dictator Saddam Hussein was quickly defeated.

OGE Drilling, Inc. of Midland, Texas, got the job of making sure the first four companies––three from America and one from Canada––worked well together. Bechtel Group set up the pipeline from the Persian Gulf that would pump sea water to the fires. Paul King, the manager for OGE Drilling at the site, said the job would mean "only TV, cards, and work, work,

work seven days a week." There was no time to waste.

In the beginning, most of the hellfighters were tough Texans and Louisianans who pronounced the word fire as "far" and called the worst blazes the "real boogers." They were men used to taking matters into their own hands when no one else could do the job. Wild Well Control President Joe Bowden claimed that "this is really no different than any of the jobs we've ever gone to. It's just bigger."

Whether that was brag or fact, putting out the fires in a short time would have looked impossible to anyone but experts. In the spring, winds known as *khamsin* sent smoke containing chemicals and poisonous metals like arsenic, lead, and copper swirling across the skies of the Middle East.

Near the burning wells, surrounded by buried land mines, were other dangers. There was always the possibility you could be bitten by a rattlesnake.

The men had human obstacles to overcome, too. Many people had "better" ideas. Some thought the U.S. and Allied military forces should get involved by dropping "fuel-air" bombs above the wells to put them out. But the rapidly shifting khamsin winds caused that idea to be rejected.

A group of Harvard University physicists suggested that an S-shaped piece of sheet metal, called an Emmons combustor, be built around each burning well. They explained that this would create a small whirlwind of fire which would remove soot from the atmosphere. This idea was not used, either.

The "oil-patch cowboys" couldn't understand why, since they knew how to do their job, people tried to make it so complicated. "Fires are no big deal

Fires in the oil fields of Kuwait continued to burn while experts discussed the best way to put out the flames.

to us," said Brian Krause, one of the first hellfighters on the job.

Some critics complained about how much the hellfighters would make putting out the well fires. The hellfighter companies charged $500,000 a month for each team of eight men. Those men worked twelve-hour days, twenty-eight days in a row, with a four-week rest between shifts. Every man made eight hundred dollars a day and up. Raymond Henry, the executive vice-president of Red Adair, Inc., had this to say about the costs: "If you think experts are expensive, try calling an amateur."

Ignoring everything but their jobs, the hellfighters set about putting out the fires, or "snuffin' and cappin'," as they called it. This is how they snuffed and capped the fires:

First, under a constant spray of sea water pumped in from the Persian Gulf, a crane mounted on a bulldozer moved in and removed debris from around the oil well. Sometimes the water alone would put out the flames, but the main purpose of the spray was to cool the men, equipment, and well itself.

Secondly, on tougher fires, a barrel filled with explosives was lifted by a crane in the area between the bottom of the flame and the place where the oil emerged from the ground, called the "wellhead." Then the crane operator ran behind a shield and lit the explosives electronically.

Finally, the explosion sucked all the oxygen away from the fire, smothering it. The crane would then lower a mechanism called a "Christmas tree" (basically, a tall bunch of valves put together). The "Christmas tree" would then be attached to the well. The valves would slowly be closed, stopping the flow of oil and finishing the job.

The trouble was, every well was unique. The Iraqi demolition experts had placed enough explosives to blow up an office building around each well. However, they had blown up each well differently. Every well was a new challenge.

Chapter 4

Hellfighters were used to losing men in fires but continued in spite of the dangers. The team from Wild Well Control led by "Big Joe" Bowden had capped more than a dozen wells by the end of March. His team included his two sons, Joe Jr. and Sam.

But in 1983, "Big Joe" lost three men in two separate gas well accidents, including his son-in-law. "They died doing what they wanted to do," Bowden said. Bowden and Joe Jr. suffered second- and third-degree burns in another gas fire.

This constant threat of danger taught hellfighters to put everything out of their minds but the job at hand, sort of like mind over matter. As American hellfighter Larry Arnold explained it, "If you don't think about gettin' hot and keep your mind on the job, you're okay. Like the guy who walks across hot coals—he ain't thinkin' about burnin' his feet. To him, those coals are clover. Same thing."

The dangerous work made a hellfighter's personal life difficult. "Boots" Hansen of Boots & Coots had been divorced three times by the time the Kuwaiti fires started. His job was more important to him than anything else. "I'm never gonna change," Boots said. "This is all I know."

As the fires were put out, rivalries between the companies began heating up. A board was put up in Kuwait City's International Hotel to keep track of which company was putting out the most well fires.

By the time summer came around, Canada's Safety Boss had pulled ahead of all other companies. Eventually, they put out 180 wells, with no one else even coming close in number of fires put out.

One explanation was that Safety Boss had developed methods using only ten percent of the water used by the Texas companies, which came in handy in a desert like Kuwait. However, James Tuppen of Boots & Coots said that Safety Boss was only hired to handle the smaller hot spots.

The Kuwaiti government correctly figured that competition would speed the plugging of the wells. Eventually, teams from twenty-seven countries joined the fire fight. A team from Hungary brought in a machine called "Big Wind." It featured Russian MiG-21 jet engines mounted on T-34 tanks to put out the flames.

But when the totals were added up, the original three teams from Texas and one team from Canada had put out over eighty percent of the fires.

All in all, the Iraqis had blown up 1,164 of Kuwait's 1,250 wells. Seven hundred thirty-two were in Kuwait, and another 432 were in a neutral zone between Kuwait and Saudi Arabia. Luckily, only 633 wells actually caught on fire.

In the beginning, people had hoped that each fire would take five days to put out, which meant the original four companies could do the job in about two years. Other people figured the job would take seven years.

Some scientists, like Carl Sagan of Cornell University, predicted terrible results for Earth, no matter how quickly the fires were put out. Climatologist Michael C. MacCraken, who studies climates for a living, said the fires would produce a cloud of pollution only "about as severe as that found on a bad day at the Los Angeles airport."

The truth was not known when the

fire fighting began, and scientists' opinions really did not matter. After all, scientists were not the ones putting out the fires, and their opinions did not speed up the process of putting out the flames.

Red Adair appeared at a hearing before the United States Senate environmental committee on June 11, 1991. He told the senators the simple facts. One hundred fifty wells had been shut off by that time, but those were "the easy ones," according to Red.

"The real hard work hasn't started," he said. He continued by saying that unless the firefighters got more support from Washington, the job would take four to five years, not the one year that some Kuwaiti officials were predicting.

To help speed up the process and get rid of the land mines, an inventor and weapons engineer named William Wattenburg suggested pulling a chain net with huge digging knives behind a

34

helicopter to explode the hidden land mines around the wells. Since some of the mines were under oil or water, and made of plastic explosives, they could not be detected by metal detectors. Sterling A. Colgate, a physicist, suggested using a small jet engine like a giant leaf blower to blast the mines out of the way, moving dirt at the rate of one thousand cubic feet a minute.

Other scientists suggested using satellite infrared images to spot the mines, the same way buried ancient cities have been found from space.

These discussions were taking place in the United States. The Kuwaiti government, though, hired a British firm called Royal Ordnance to clear the mines. Royal Ordnance workers used old methods like walking along the sand, probing with hand-held rods to find the mines. Even with scientific theories and high technology, it all came down to people who could do the job.

Red Adair was promised the added support he requested, and the hellfighters kept at it, day by day, well by well. Then, on the day after Red testified before the Senate, a team of scientists released a report about the effect of the Kuwaiti oil field fires.

Chapter 5

Twenty-seven scientists from the Washington-based National Science Foundation had conducted surveys from the air over Kuwait from May 16 to June 12, 1991. They made thirty-five flights at altitudes of as much as twenty-two thousand feet. The scientists reported that the smoke blanket from the fires was large enough to stretch from New York City to the tip of Florida. The smoke was one hundred miles wide.

Luckily, there was also good news. The smoke was being absorbed by clouds and would fall back to the ground as rain. Lawrence Radke, co-leader of the team, said that the smoke would have to stay in the atmosphere for several months and move up to the stratosphere before it could affect the global climate. That could cause world temperatures to drop by blocking out the rays of the sun.

Other scientists, though, weren't so sure. Adam Tromby is a British physicist and climatologist who visited the Persian Gulf region that June. He said that people in Dhahran, Saudi Arabia, were experiencing nausea, headaches, and shortness of breath. If only one percent of the smoke reached the stratosphere, it would cause a temperature drop of several degrees for years.

By then, 175 well fires had been put out, but there was no way to predict when the entire job would be completed.

"It's a disaster that staggers the imagination," said Brian McCutcheon of Safety Boss. "Even for guys who've worked on spectacular fires."

To help hurry things along, Safety Boss used different methods than the Texas hellfighters. Their main firefighting method was to spray *potassium bicarbonate* (a dry chemical compound that resembles baking soda) onto the blazing wells at a rate of two hundred pounds per second. Whether or not these were "easy" wells as Boots & Coots claimed, it worked.

Red Adair & Company, Wild Well Control, and Boots & Coots used older, tried-and-true methods. They dug reservoirs in the sand near each well. The reservoirs could hold up to a million gallons of sea water. They would then pump four streams of water onto a well at once from different directions. This could usually put out a fire in half an hour. If that failed, they exploded dynamite (in an insulated barrel) over the flames to snuff out the fire.

Despite the firefighters' efforts, many of the Kuwaiti oil fields continued to burn. Some wells burned for nearly a year. More than four million barrels of oil were burned daily.

Even with the flames out, the job was far from easy. The roar of the escaping oil could be deafening even to the hellfighter wearing standard earplugs. The job was also very dangerous despite hard hats, goggles, and protective equipment.

Even if a burning well was put out, there was always the chance the wellhead could explode. If you yelled for help and no one was looking your way, you might be out of luck.

"You've got oil flowing out of a pipe at eight hundred miles an hour," McCutcheon said. "That's a powerful stream of oil."

Every hellfighter on the job, whether he was wearing the red coveralls of Red Adair & Company, the white ones of Boots & Coots, or the yellow ones with black trim of Wild Well Control, ended up each day completely soaked with thick oil. If the sun was out all day, that meant walking around in oil-soaked coveralls in 120-degree heat. There was always the chance you could fall over from the heat and die before someone could get to you to help.

"Every day I'm in that field," one roughneck said, "I find three or four new ways to die."

In the language of hellfighters, new firefighters are called "worms." Those who prove they can do the job are called "hands" or "firefighters." Those who can't make it are called "gonsels." Instead of being fired, they are "run off."

In Kuwait, there were no "worms" or "gonsels" to run off, only "hands." Each one of them worked extremely hard to cap the burning wells. Only they didn't call it capping. They called it "killing" a fire.

By mid-summer 1991, with the desert sun blazing hotter than ever, there were still a lot of wells left to "kill." It looked like the job might take years to finish.

Chapter 6

While the hellfighters were fighting the fires, scientists were working overtime to predict what would happen to the environment. The Max Planck Institute for Meteorology put together a computer model that suggested the smoke would soon cover most of Russia, a large portion of Europe, about a third of Africa, most of India, and all of North and South Korea by February 1992.

Investigators for the National Oceanic and Atmospheric Administration in the United States said they had taken samples of soot from the Kuwaiti fires at the Mauna Loa Observatory atop a high mountain in Hawaii. Did Saddam

Hussein help cause the thinner ozone layer, global warming, and increased acid rain?

Although President George Bush put together a task force headed by the Environmental Protection Agency to study what was happening, very little information had resulted. Or, if the task force discovered anything, it wasn't saying much to reporters. The United States did not want the world to know about this pollution.

Some scientists had predicted that the smoke might prevent the heavy rains, or monsoons, in India from occurring that year. Millions of people who depend on the rain for their crops could starve.

However, the opposite had occurred. The monsoons had come right on time, including one huge typhoon (hurricane) on May 1, 1991. It hit a costal region and killed one hundred thousand people.

Tiruvalam Krishnamurti, an expert on monsoons from Florida State University, suggested that since the storm was accompanied by unusually high flooding—two feet higher than ever before—there might have been a link to the Kuwaiti fires. He believed this because raindrops usually form around dust and soot particles in the air, causing more rains. After the Kuwaiti oil field fires, there was plenty of soot and dust in the air.

Soviet scientists reported that higher levels of acid rain than ever before had been falling in southern Russia. Satellite images showed smoke and darkened snow in Pakistan and northern India.

A new danger had arisen in Kuwait. Pockets of gasses had formed underneath the pools of oil on the desert. People had been killed trying to drive across shallow pools when sparks from their vehicles lit the hidden gasses and caused an explosion.

While the scientists made their computer models and reports and discussed possibilities, the hellfighters kept fighting. With autumn came a surprise—they were running ahead of schedule!

The original date set by Kuwaiti officials for extinguishing all the fires was March 1992. One report said that all the fires would be extinguished by November of 1991. Abdullah al-Gabandi, the managing director of the Kuwait Investment Authority, told reporters that 631 of the original fires had been put out as of Tuesday, October 15.

Finally, only two wells remained to be extinguished, but they resisted the best efforts of all the hellfighters. The firefighters put aside any differences they might have had. A great combined effort again resulted in "killing" the last two wells.

46

On November 7, 1991, the effort to put out the fires in Kuwait finally ended. The Emir of Kuwait flicked a remote-control switch that sealed the last well. (Actually, the well had already been put out. The 150-foot high column of fire extinguished by the Emir at the ceremony had been re-lit for the occasion.)

Hundreds of oil lakes still remained on the desert. Kuwaiti officials said they had paid $1.5 billion to have the fires put out. Western oil officials estimated that the cost was really $2 billion. Kuwait Oil Minister Hamoud Abdulla al-Raqba claimed that by capping the wells three months ahead of schedule, the country had saved $12 billion.

At that time, Kuwait's wells were already back to pumping oil at the rate of three hundred thousand barrels a day. Before the wells were set on fire by Saddam Hussein's army, they had produced two million barrels a day.

The fires were out. By United Nations order, the Iraqi government had to pay for all the damage done by releasing oil into the Persian Gulf and by burning Kuwaiti oil fields. But while the Gulf War and the war against the "devil's forest fire" were over, another war was starting.

Those involved in the battle for the environment held international meetings to figure out what needed to be done. They discovered little had been done. While environmental groups like Friends of the Earth were greatly concerned about what would happen to the environment of Kuwait as a result of the oil well fires, others were not so upset.

David Usher, president of the Spill Control Association of America, said, "The damage in the gulf appears to have been minimal. There have been no . . . reports of environmental damage."

Brent Blackwelder, president of Friends of the Earth, responded by saying Usher was an "ecological ignoramus." An ignoramus is a person who is ignorant or uninformed.

By April 1992, some of the pools of oil that remained in Kuwait were half a mile wide, more than a mile long, and two or three feet deep. Kuwaiti officials reported that the oil was seeping into the soil, killing plants, birds, and insects. Strong fumes from the lakes were causing lung disease, coughing, and other irritations. The pollution had become the country's main worry. Perhaps the president of Friends of the Earth had been right.

The greatest fool, though, was the man who ordered the setting of the ·fires—Saddam Hussein. Hussein showed complete disregard for human life and the environment in the Persian Gulf. He ordered his army to blow up the oil wells of Kuwait purely to suit his own wishes.

There was little chance Saddam Hussein would ever fight another war like the one in the Persian Gulf. The world hoped there would never be another "devil's forest fire."

It had taken hellfighters from twenty-seven countries almost a year to put out the flames. They were all thankful it was over.

Bibliography

The Daily Breeze, April 21, 1992.

Life, "Hell on Earth," July 1991.

Maclean's, "A Desert Inferno," July 8, 1991.

The New York Times, November 12, 1991.

Newsweek, "Hellfighters to the Rescue," March 25, 1991.

People, "Fields of Fire," March 29, 1991.

Science, "To Stop Kuwait's Fires, First Clear the Mines," June 21, 1991.

Scientific American, "Up in Flames," May 1991.

Scientific American, "Burning Questions," July 1991.

Singerman, Philip. *An American Hero: The Red Adair Story.* Boston: Little, Brown and Company, 1990.

U.S. News and World Report, "Flameout," November 11, 1991.

The Wall Street Journal, October 18, 1991.

The Wall Street Journal, November 7, 1991.